Mike Piazza

Phenomenal Catcher

by
Thomas S. Owens

The Rosen Publishing Group's
PowerKids Press™
New York

Published in 1997 by The Rosen Publishing Group, Inc.
29 East 21st Street, New York, NY 10010

First Edition

Book Design: Kim Sonsky

Photo Credits: Cover, pp. 4, 7, 8, 19, 20, 21 © AP/Wide World Photos; p. 4 (inset) © Reuters/Gary Hershon/Archive Photos; p. 11 © Reuters/Joe Giza/Archive Photos; p. 12 © Richard Mackson/FPG International; p. 13 © Reuters/Adrees A. Latif/Archive Photos; p. 15 © Reuters/Ray Stubblebine/Archive Photos; p. 16 © Reuters/Gary C. Caskey/Archive Photos.

Owens, Tom, 1960–
    Mike Piazza : phenomenal catcher / Thomas S. Owens.
        p.   cm. — (Sports greats)
    Includes index.
    Summary: Profiles the popular young catcher for the Los Angeles Dodgers, who was voted National League Rookie of the Year in 1993.
    ISBN 0-8239-5089-1
    1. Piazza, Mike, 1968– —Juvenile literature. 2. Baseball players—United States—Biography—Juvenile literature. 3. Los Angeles Dodgers (Baseball team)—Juvenile literature. [1. Piazza, Mike, 1968–
2. Baseball players.] I. Title. II. Series: Sports greats (New York, N.Y.)
GV865.P52095 1997
796.357'092—dc21   97-506
[B]   CIP
                                                                                                                        AC

Manufactured in the United States of America

Contents

1 Young Mike 5

2 Mike Piazza's Start 6

3 A Special Friend 9

4 Piazza the Player 10

5 The Dodgers Call 13

6 The Power of Piazza 14

7 Working Together 17

8 Famous in Japan 18

9 Mike and Mike 21

10 Mike at Home 22

Glossary 23

Index 24

Young Mike

Vincent Piazza and his seven-year-old son, Mike, went to the 1976 All-Star Game. Each year, fans vote for the players they want to play in the All-Star Game. The 1976 game was held at Veterans Stadium—the home of the Philadelphia Phillies. The Piazzas love baseball. They had season tickets for the Phillies' games. That meant they could go to all the Phillies' home games. Young Mike went to the All-Star Game to watch another Mike—Mike Schmidt, the Phillies' star third baseman.

That night, Mike Piazza dreamed about the All-Star Game. Would he ever meet Mike Schmidt? Would he play in the **major leagues** (MAY-jer LEEGZ) too? Would he ever be in an All-Star Game?

◀ Mike Piazza once went to the ballpark to watch his hero, Mike Schmidt, play baseball. Twenty years later, Mike Schmidt (inset) was watching Mike Piazza catch with the Dodgers.

Mike Piazza's Start

Mike Piazza grew up wanting to play major league baseball. Mike's father wanted his son to be happy. He built an indoor batting cage for Mike.

When Mike was twelve, his father met Ted Williams. Ted was a great Red Sox hitter who played from 1939 to 1960. He was voted into the Baseball Hall of Fame. Ted told Mike's father he'd come to see his son practice hitting. Even though Mike was young, Ted said Mike's swing was special.

Former Red Sox hitter Ted Williams knew that ▶
Mike could be a great hitter too someday.

A Special Friend

Mike's family had other friends involved in baseball. Mike's father was a distant cousin of Tommy Lasorda, the manager of the Los Angeles Dodgers. When the Dodgers came to Philadelphia, near Mike's home, Tommy let eleven-year-old Mike be the team's batboy. Sometimes Tommy pitched to Mike, letting him practice batting with the Dodgers. He watched Mike grow as a boy and a player. As he spent more time with **professional** (pro-FESH-un-ul) players, Mike's dream to be a major league player grew too.

◀ Tommy Lasorda helped Mike's dream of becoming a major league player come true.

9

Piazza the Player

Mike played basketball in a youth **league** (LEEG) for a year, but he wasn't very good at it. He scored only four points all season. He decided to quit basketball, but he stuck with baseball.

Mike played baseball in high school. Each year he tried out for the **varsity** (VAR-sih-tee) team, but he didn't make it until eleventh grade. He soon broke the school's record for hitting the most home runs. After high school, Mike went to the University of Miami. He played baseball there, but only batted nine times. He moved to a community college, where he played well.

Mike had to work hard to play baseball well enough to make it to the major leagues. ▶

The Dodgers Call

In 1988, Tommy Lasorda asked the Dodgers to choose Mike as one of their **draft** (DRAFT) picks. With their last draft pick, the Dodgers chose Mike.

Mike had been a first baseman in high school. But because he wasn't a fast runner, Mike switched to playing catcher in the **minor leagues** (MY-ner LEEGZ). By 1993, he moved up to start with the Dodgers. Although he was the Dodgers' last pick, Mike proved that he was talented. He became an All-Star, then the National League **Rookie** (ROOH-kee) of the Year. His 35 home runs set a record for rookie catchers. The Dodgers had a new hitting star.

◀ As the 1,390th out of 1,433 players chosen in the draft, Mike was nearly the last player picked.

The Power of Piazza

Fans watched Mike get better every year. In his four years in the major leagues, Mike had been chosen every year as a player in the annual All-Star Game. He finished every season batting at least .300, and he batted in at least 90 runs each year. Most importantly, he played in 100 or more games every season. That's not easy for catchers, who get injured a lot when base runners bang into them. Some fans wanted Mike to move to a safer job, such as first baseman. They didn't want the team's top hitter to be hurt. But who could catch as well as Mike?

Mike wasn't afraid of being hurt by the runners who ▶
sometimes slammed into him at home base.

Working Together

When Japanese pitching star Hideo Nomo joined the Dodgers in 1995, Mike became "his" catcher. They worked closely together. At first, they spoke different languages. But they learned to **communicate** (kuh-MYOON-ih-kayt). If Hideo was upset on the pitching mound after a bad pitch, Mike would stop the game and run out to the mound to talk to him. Mike would pretend to be upset too. He would try to say an angry word in Japanese. Hideo would laugh at Mike speaking such words in his language. Then he would feel good enough to pitch again. With Mike's help, Hideo became Rookie of the Year.

◀ Mike helped Hideo play his best on the field.

17

Famous in Japan

Hideo told Japanese **reporters** (ree-POR-terz) how Mike helped him. Fans in Japan thought of Hideo and Mike as a team. Mike became famous in Japan. He made a Japanese **commercial** (kuh-MER-shul) selling underwear. A company that makes construction equipment hired Mike for commercials too. This company claimed that their machines were as powerful as Mike. In November 1996, members of different major league teams played against Japanese baseball stars. Many of Mike's Japanese fans were there, cheering him on.

Just before the game in Japan, the construction company that Mike did commercials for gave him a tractor! ▶

Just Meet
KOMATSU
Just Meet
KOMATSU
Just Meet
KOMATSU
Just Meet
KOMATSU
Just Meet
KOMATSU
Just Meet
KOMATSU
Dodgers
31

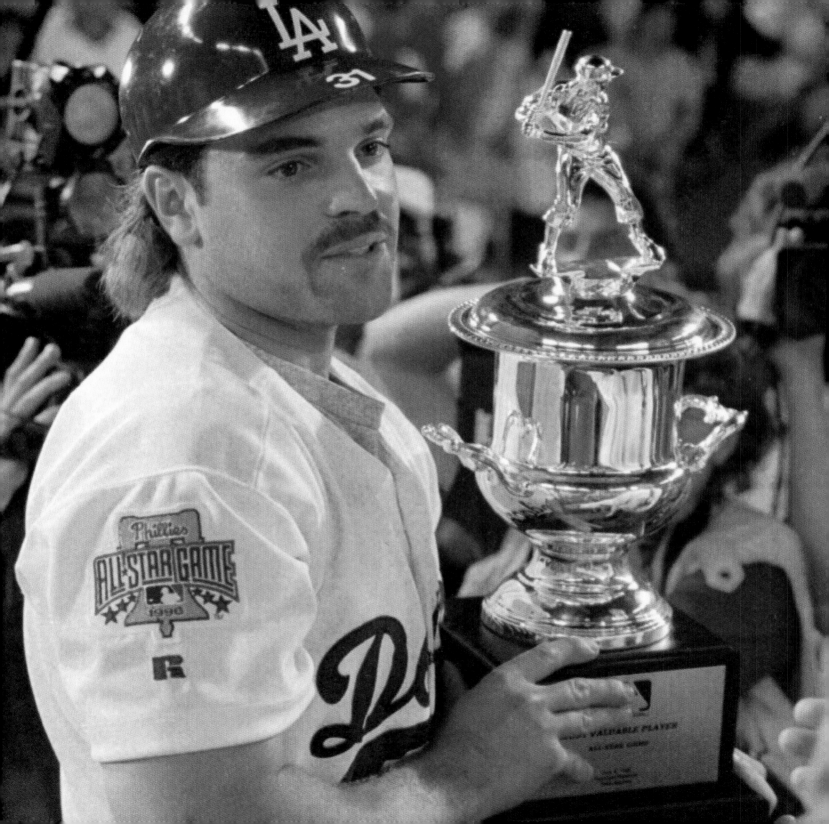

Mike and Mike

Mike Piazza went on to become more than a major league player. In 1996, the star catcher for the Dodgers was again chosen to play in the All-Star Game. This time the game was in Philadelphia, near where Mike grew up. The pre-game "first pitch" was thrown to Mike by his hero, Mike Schmidt. Twenty years before, Mike had watched Mike Schmidt from the stands. Now they shook hands as Mike Piazza's father watched.

Mike Piazza's two hits helped his team win the game. Mike was voted Most **Valuable** (VAL-yoo-bul) Player, or MVP. Mike Schmidt, Mike's boyhood hero, **autographed** (AW-toh-graft) a baseball for Mike Piazza. "You're the best," he wrote. Who's the hero now?

◄ Mike has proven to himself, his teammates, and his fans that he is a major league player.

Mike at Home

Even when this catcher isn't behind home plate, he feels "safe" at home. He loves to play the drums. Heavy metal bands have let Mike play the drums at their concerts. He is a hockey fan, and he likes to watch old movies. Besides being in many TV commercials, Mike has acted on shows that he likes, such as *Beverly Hills 90210*.

Mike also keeps learning. He bought a computer in 1996 to learn about the Internet. He's reading books again that he didn't like as a college student. As a baseball player and as a person, Mike keeps working to better himself.

Glossary

autograph (AW-toh-graf) When a person writes his or her name.

commercial (kuh-MER-shul) A message selling something on television or the radio that is played during and between programs.

communicate (kuh-MYOON-ih-kayt) To share information or news with someone.

draft (DRAFT) A time during which professional teams take turns choosing new players from colleges, high schools, and other countries.

league (LEEG) An organization of sports teams.

major league (MAY-jer LEEG) Top-level professional baseball teams.

minor league (MY-ner LEEG) Lower-level professional baseball teams.

professional (pro-FESH-un-ul) A person who is paid to do something.

reporter (ree-POR-ter) A person who gathers and gives information for a newspaper, magazine, or radio or television station.

rookie (ROOH-kee) A first-year player.

valuable (VAL-yoo-bul) Someone or something that is worth a lot.

varsity (VAR-sih-tee) The highest team in a school sport.

Index

A
All-Star Game, 5, 13, 14, 21

B
Baseball Hall of Fame, 6
basketball, 10
batboy, 9
batting cage, 6

C
catcher, 13, 14, 17, 21, 22
commercial, 18, 22

D
drums, 22

F
first baseman, 13, 14

J
Japan, 18
Japanese, 17, 18

L
Lasorda, Tommy, 9, 13
Los Angeles Dodgers, 9, 13, 17, 21

M
major league, 5, 6, 9, 14, 18, 21
minor league, 13
Most Valuable Player, 21

N
Nomo, Hideo, 17, 18

P
Philadelphia Phillies, 5
Piazza, Vincent, 5

R
Red Sox, 6
Rookie of the Year, 13, 17

S
Schmidt, Mike, 5, 21

U
University of Miami, 10

V
varsity, 10

W
Williams, Ted, 6